Table Of Content

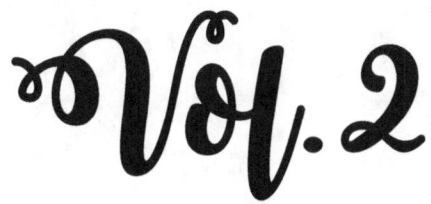
Vol.2

What is Lettering?

Lettering can be simply defined as
"the art of drawing letters".
A lot goes into making lettering look right,
and that's an entirely different topic,
but the concept is very simple:
a specific combination of letterforms crafted
for a single use and purpose as opposed to
using previously designed letters
as components, as with typography.

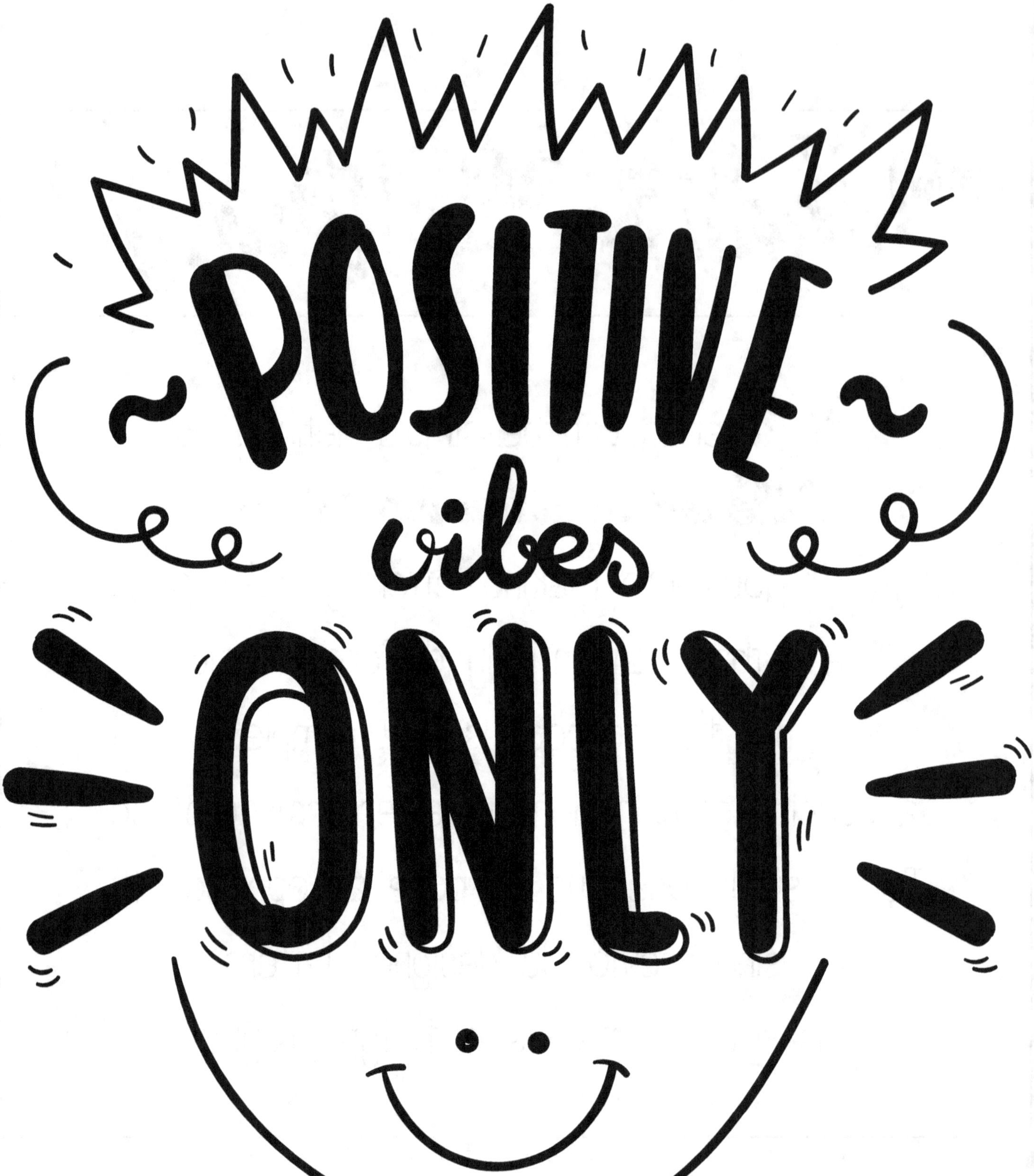
POSITIVE
vibes
ONLY

Study of Font Styles

SERIF

Serifs are the small lines tailing from the edge of letters and symbols, seperated into distinct unit for a typewriter or typsetter

Sans-serif is a typeface that does not have the small projecting features called "serifs" at the end stoke

SAN-SERIF

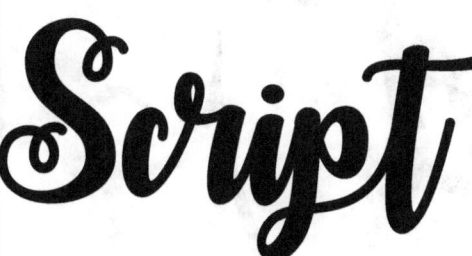

Script fonts mimic historical or modern handwriting styles. They look as if they are written with different styles of writing instruments ranging calligraphy pens to paint brushes. Typical characteristics of script type are connected or nearly connected flowing letterforms and slanted, rounded characters.

Handwritten fonts that are unofficial. Because it seems to be writing more than typing. Suitable for casual work such as hand-made or bakery.

HANDWRITTEN

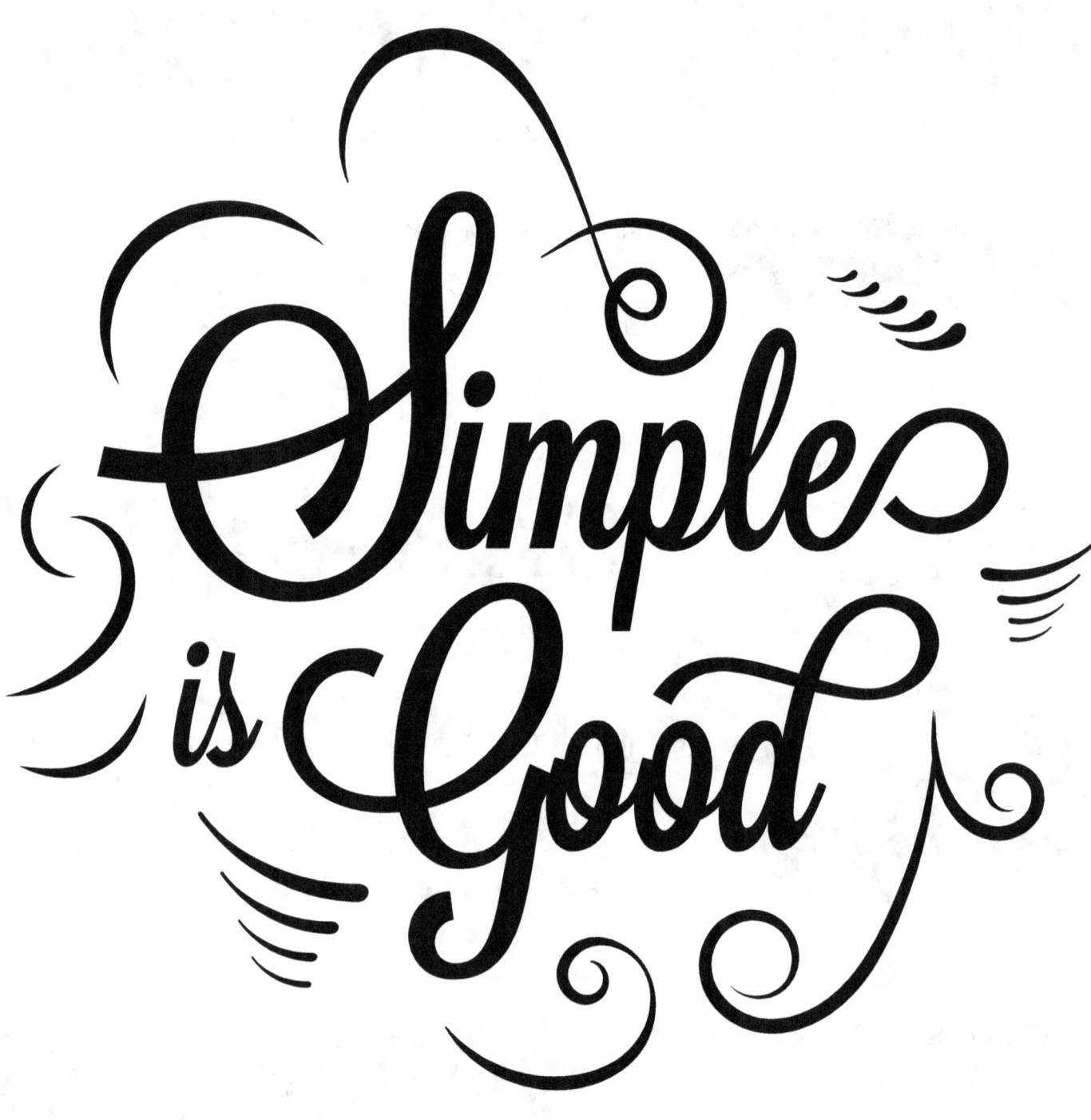

Tools and Equipment

PENCILS :
Used a plain old mechanical pencil and that works fine. The Beauty of hand lettering is that you really only need pencil to begin.

ERASER :
Erasers can be just as important as pens/pencils in developing a beautiful lettering piece!

INK PENS :
Probably the most popular pens that I see letterers use are Micron Pens, which are especially useful because they have multi-packs that have varying tip widths. Other pens are
- Uni-ball Vision Stick Fine Point Roller Ball Pen
- Uni-ball Signo
- Papermate Flair Felt Tip Pen(Medium Point)

BRUSH PENS (WATER BRUSH PEN) :
Brush Lettering has become incredibly popular in the world of lettering for its fluidity and versatility in bridging the gap between lettering and calligraphy. Recommend of Brush Pen
- TomBow Dual Brush Pens
- Pentel Color Brush
- Pilot Pocket Brush Pen
- Shapie Water-Based Poster Paint Maker
- Faber-Castell Brush Pen
- Uni Brush Pen

Start YOUR morning WITH a smile

ALPHABET DRILL 1

A A

B B

C C

D D

E E

F F

G G

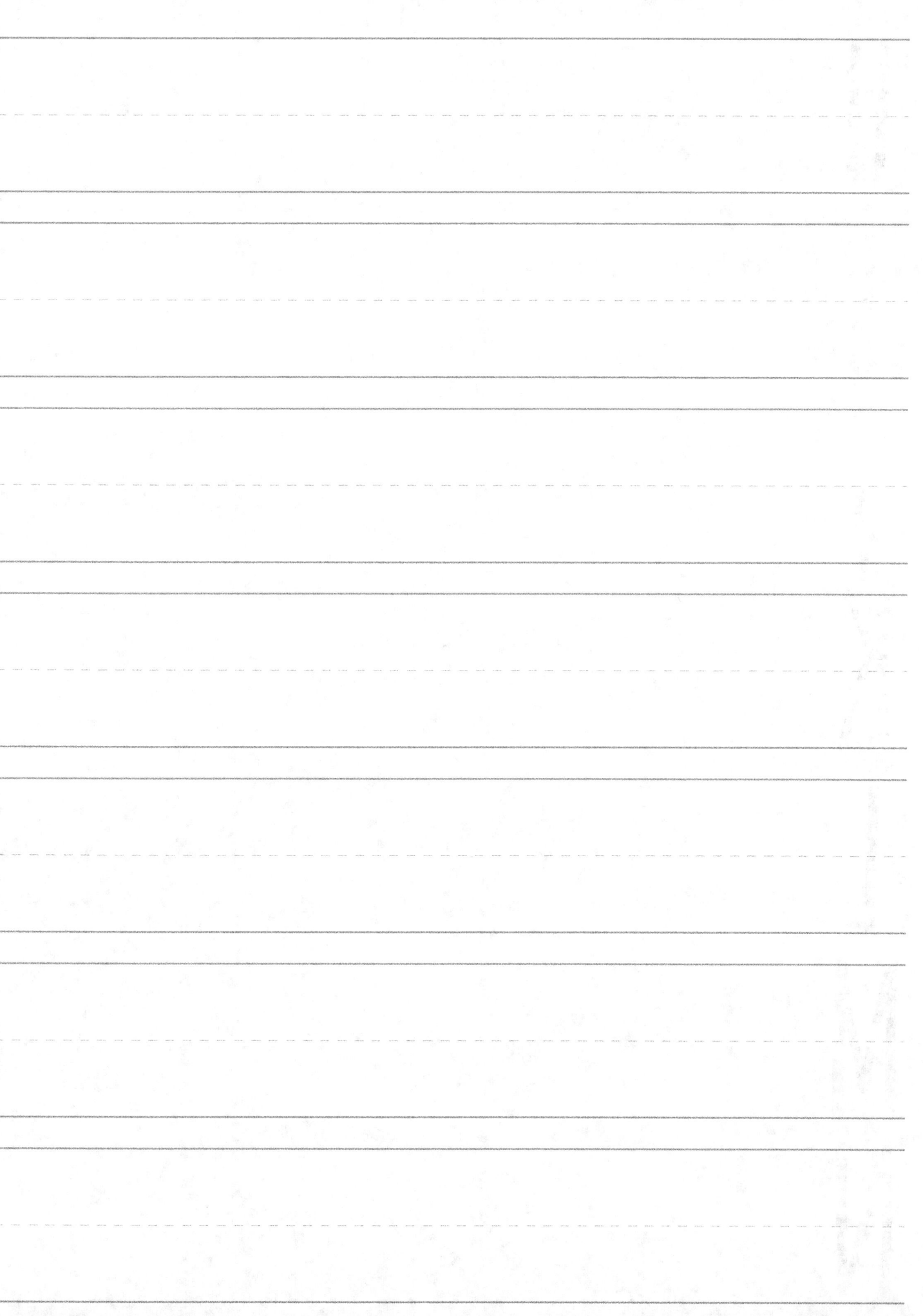

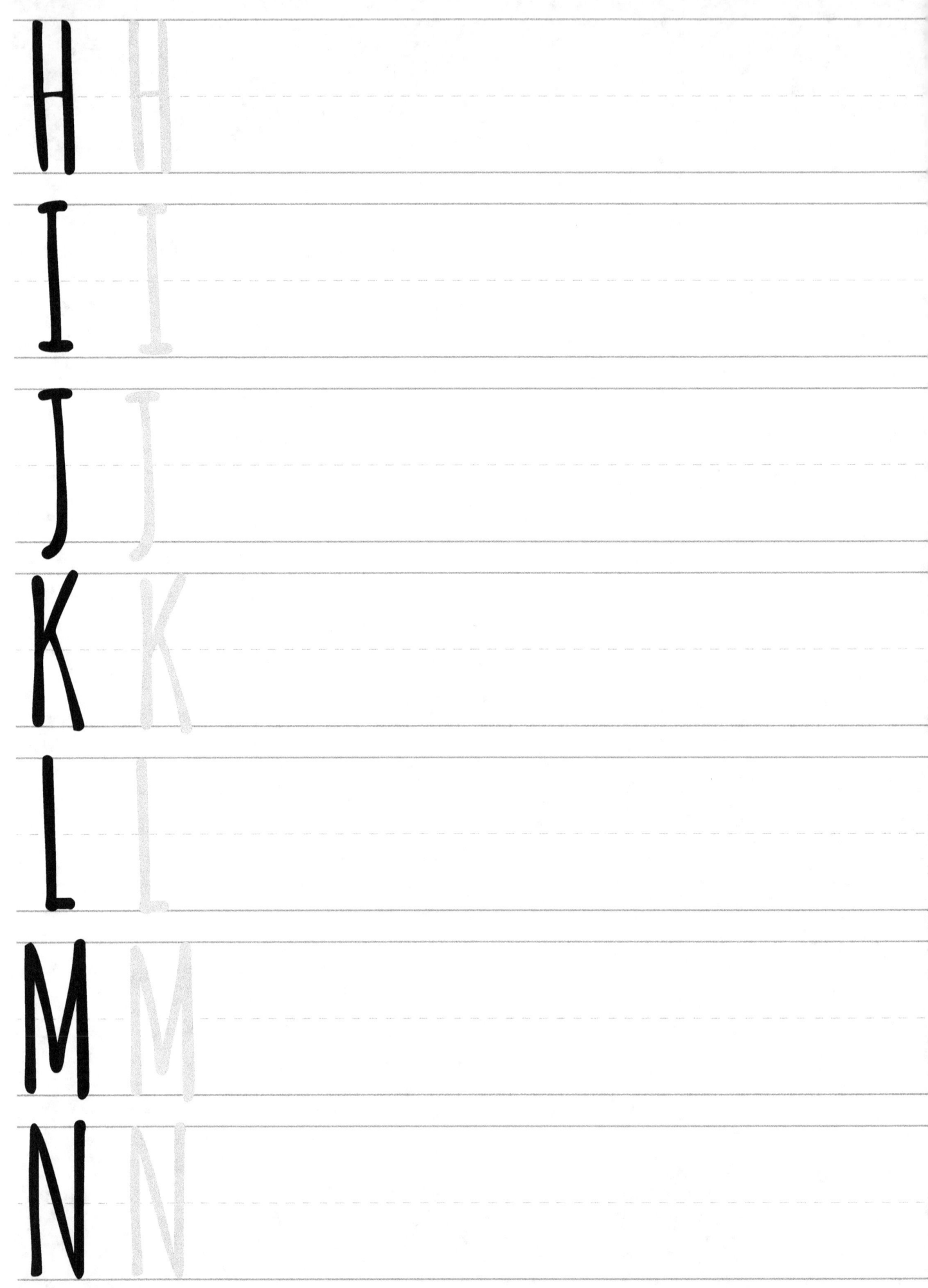

O O

P P

Q Q

R R

S S

T T

U U

V V

W W

X X

Y Y

Z Z

! !

? ?

A A

B B

C C

D D

E E

F F

G G

H H

I I

J J

K K

L L

M M

N N

O O

P P

Q Q

R R

S S

T T

U U

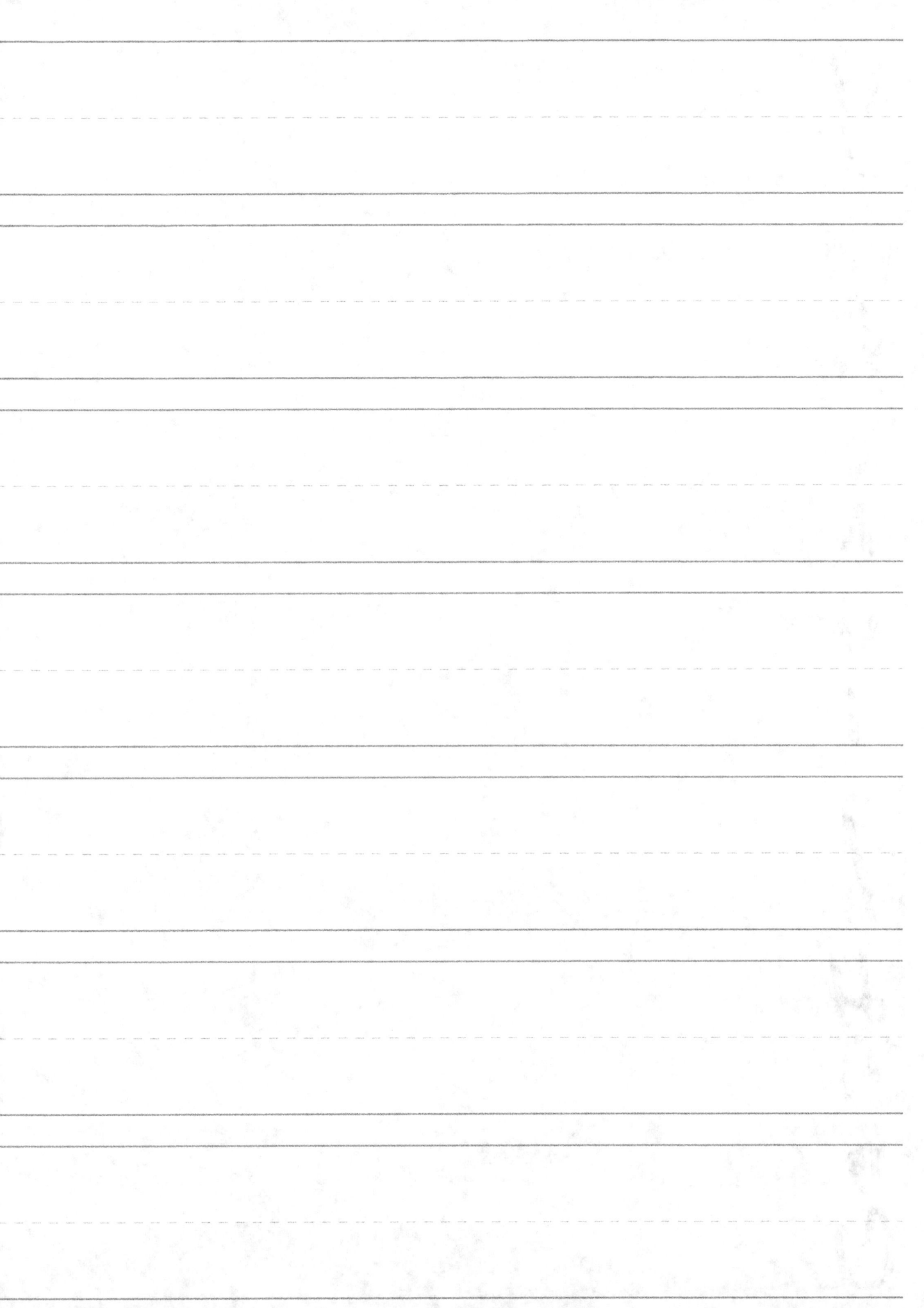

V V

W W

X X

Y Y

Z Z

# #

& &

Alphabet Drill 2

A A

B B

C C

D D

E E

F F

G G

H H H

I I I

J J J

K K K

L L L

M M M

N N N

O O O

P P P

Q Q Q

R R R

S S S

T T T

U U U

V V

W W

X X

Y Y

Z Z

! !

? ?

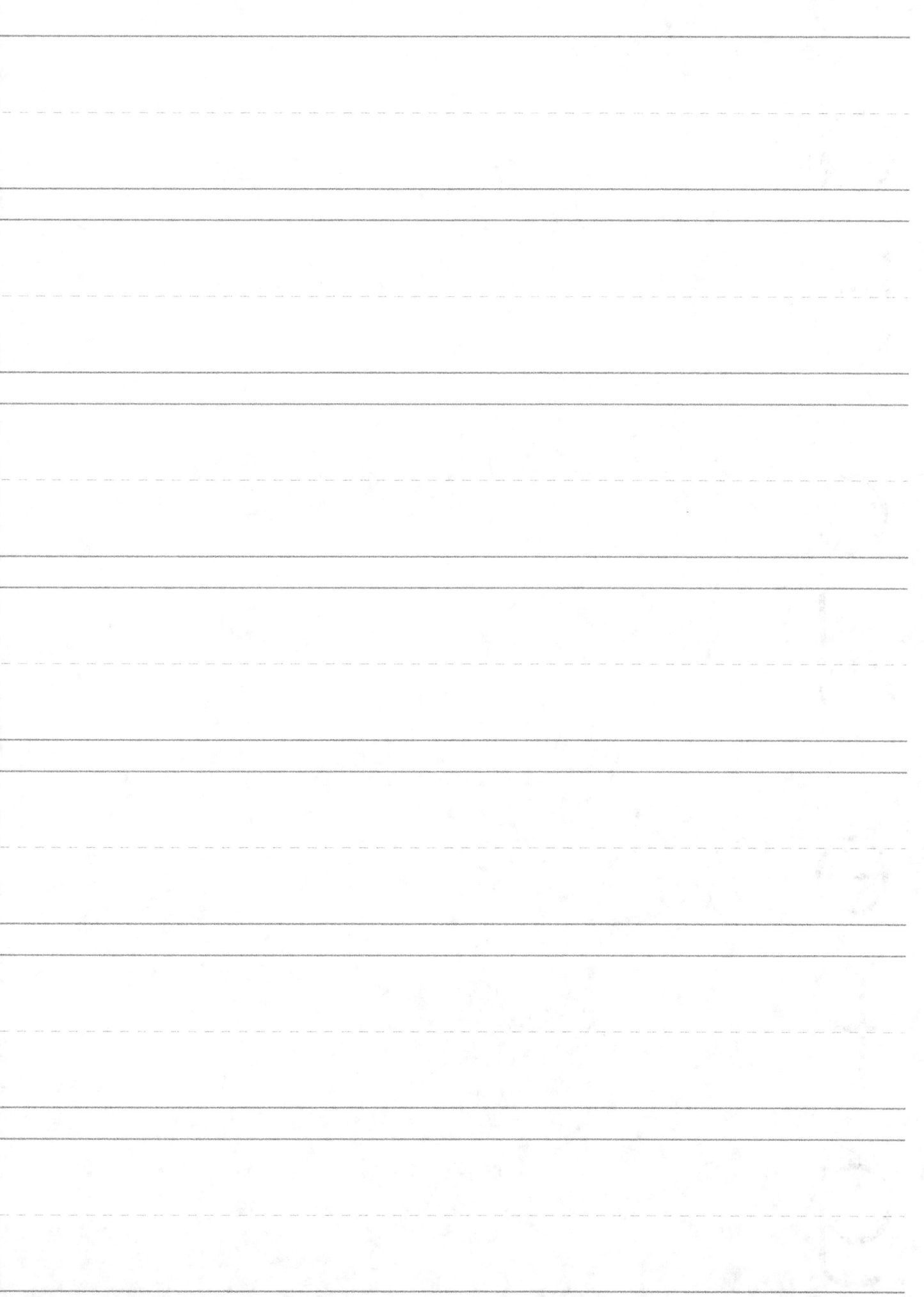

a a

b b

c c

d d

e e

f f

g g

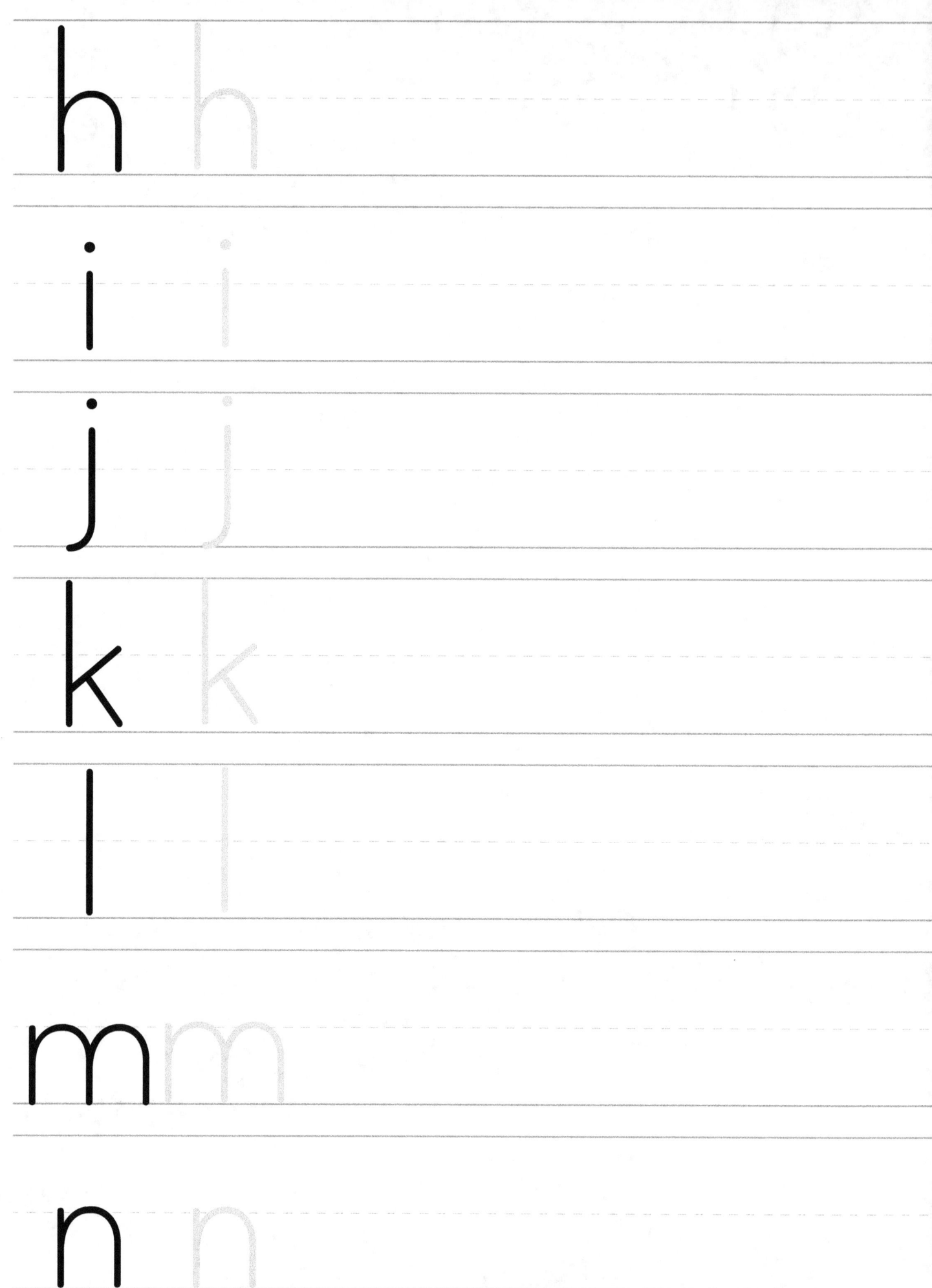

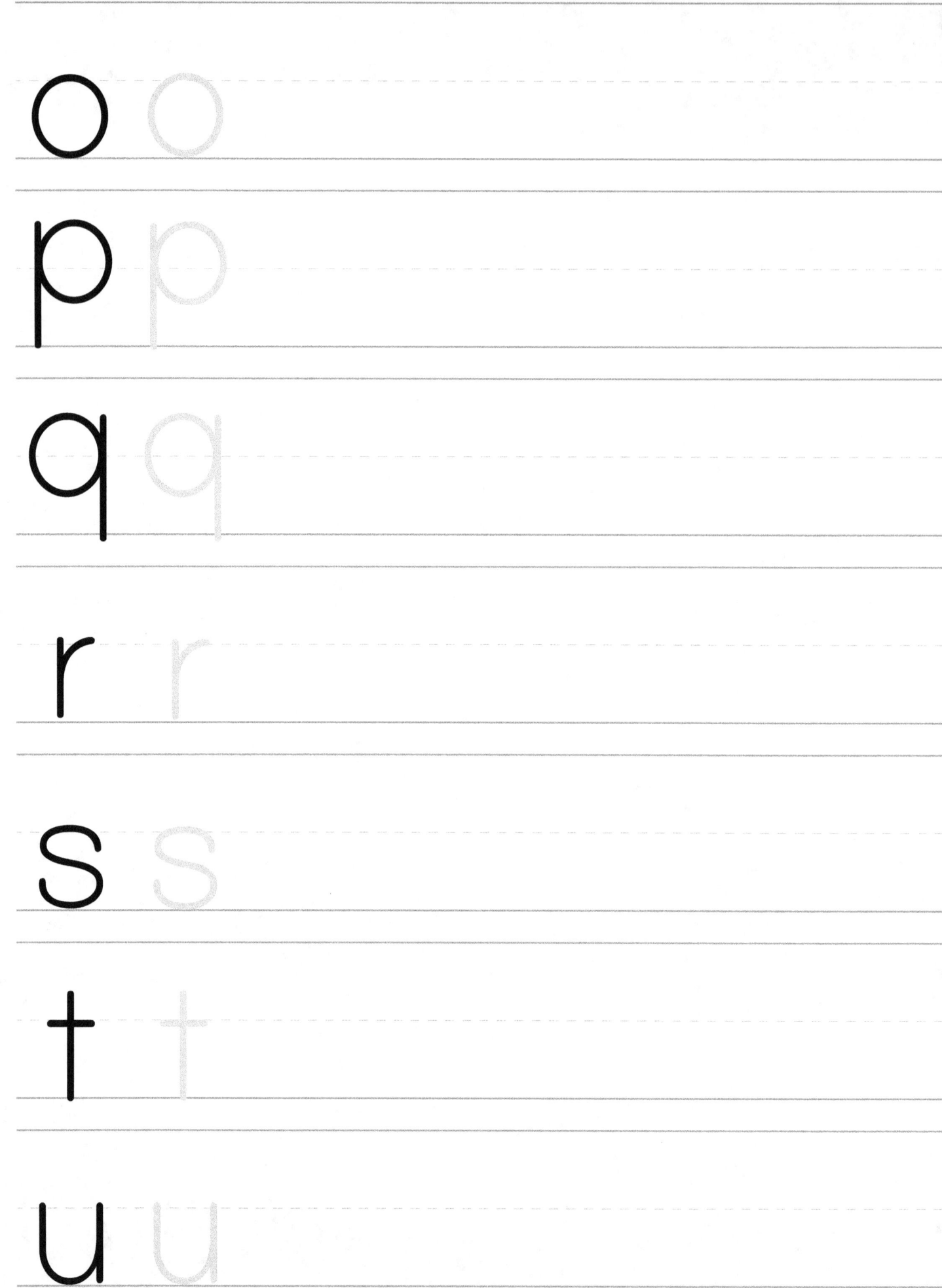

v v

w w

x x

y y

z z

# #

& &

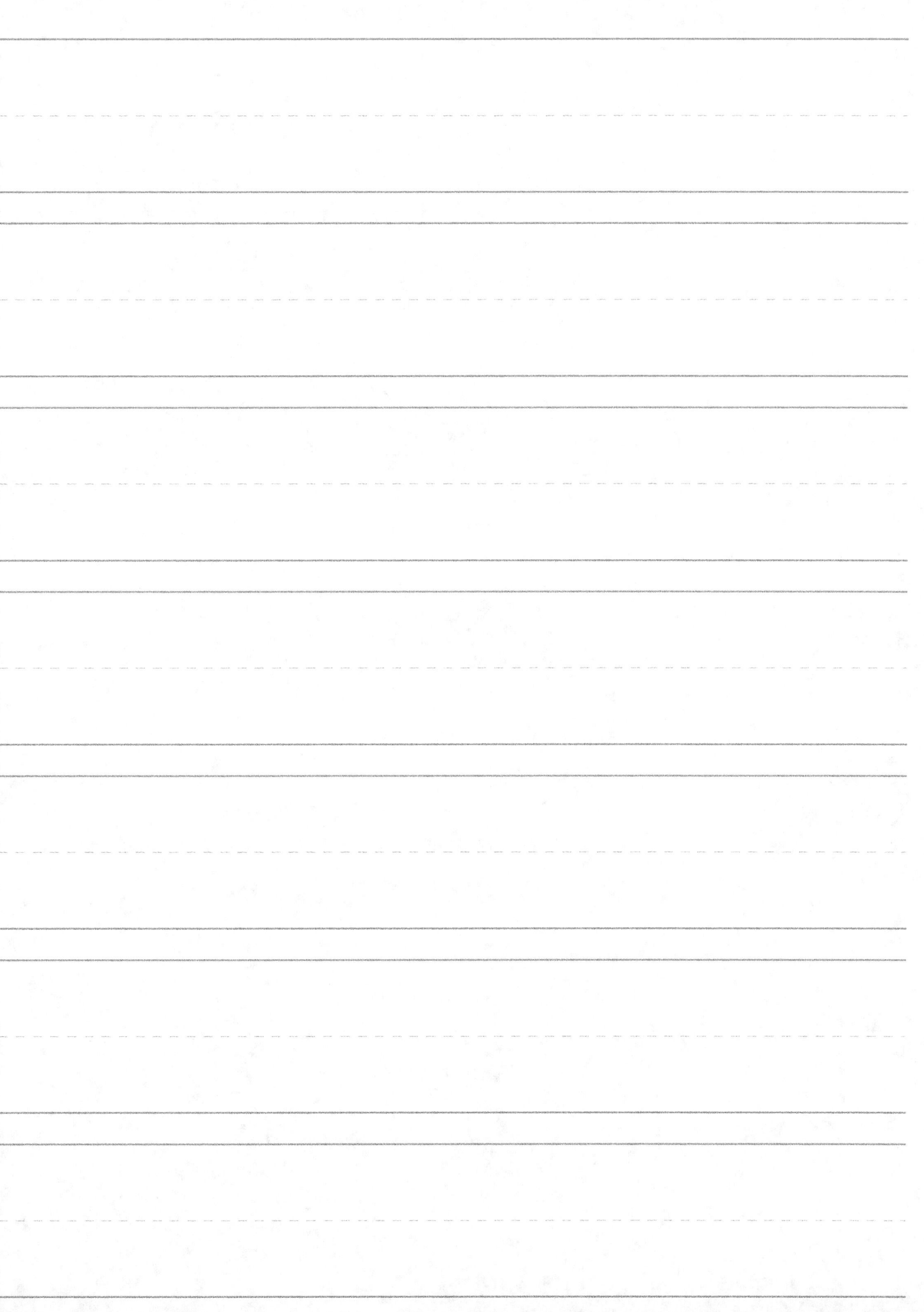

Alphabet Drill 3

A A

B B

C C

D D

E E

F F

G G

H

J

J

K

L

M

N

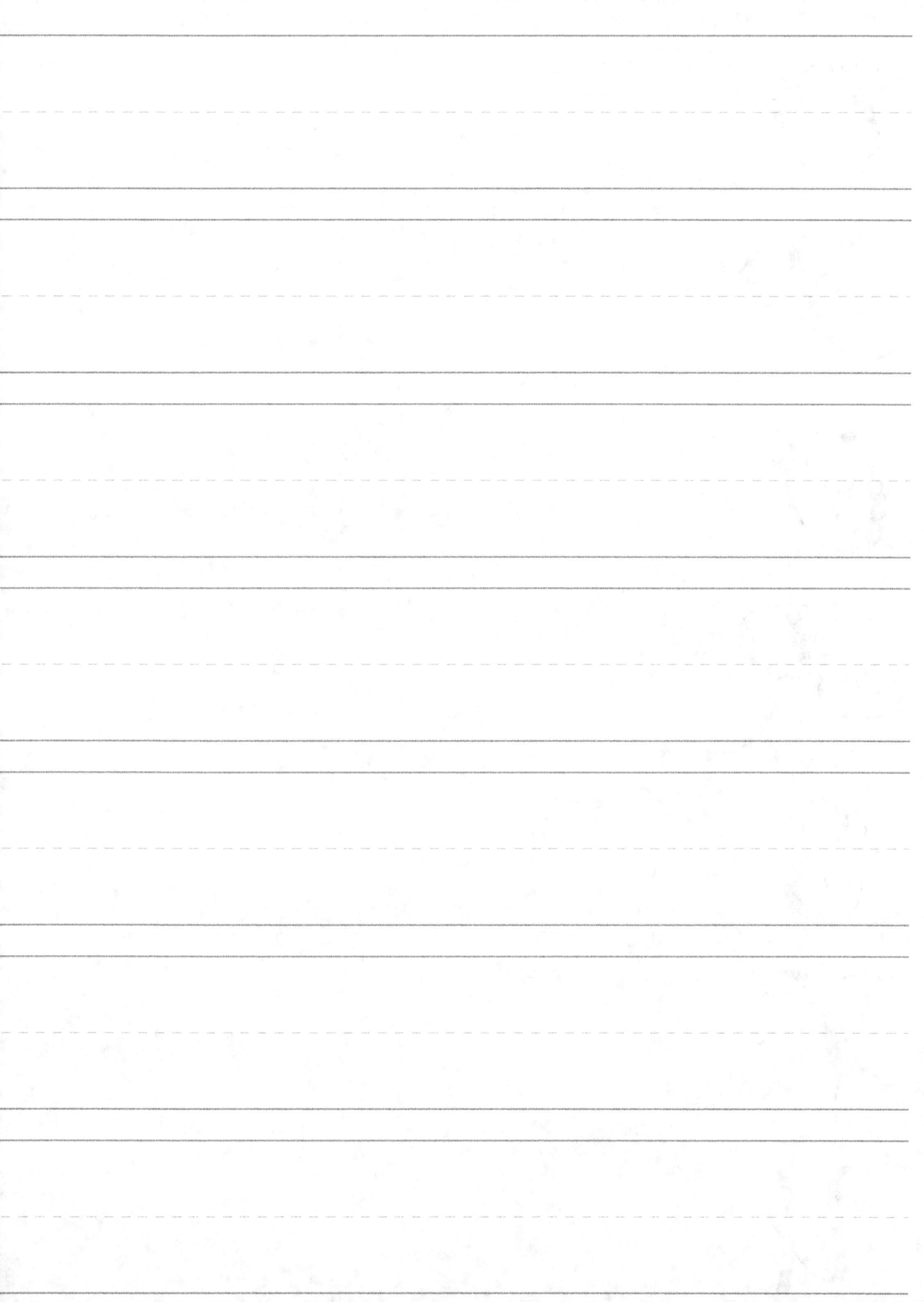

O O

P P

Q Q

R R

S S

T T

U U

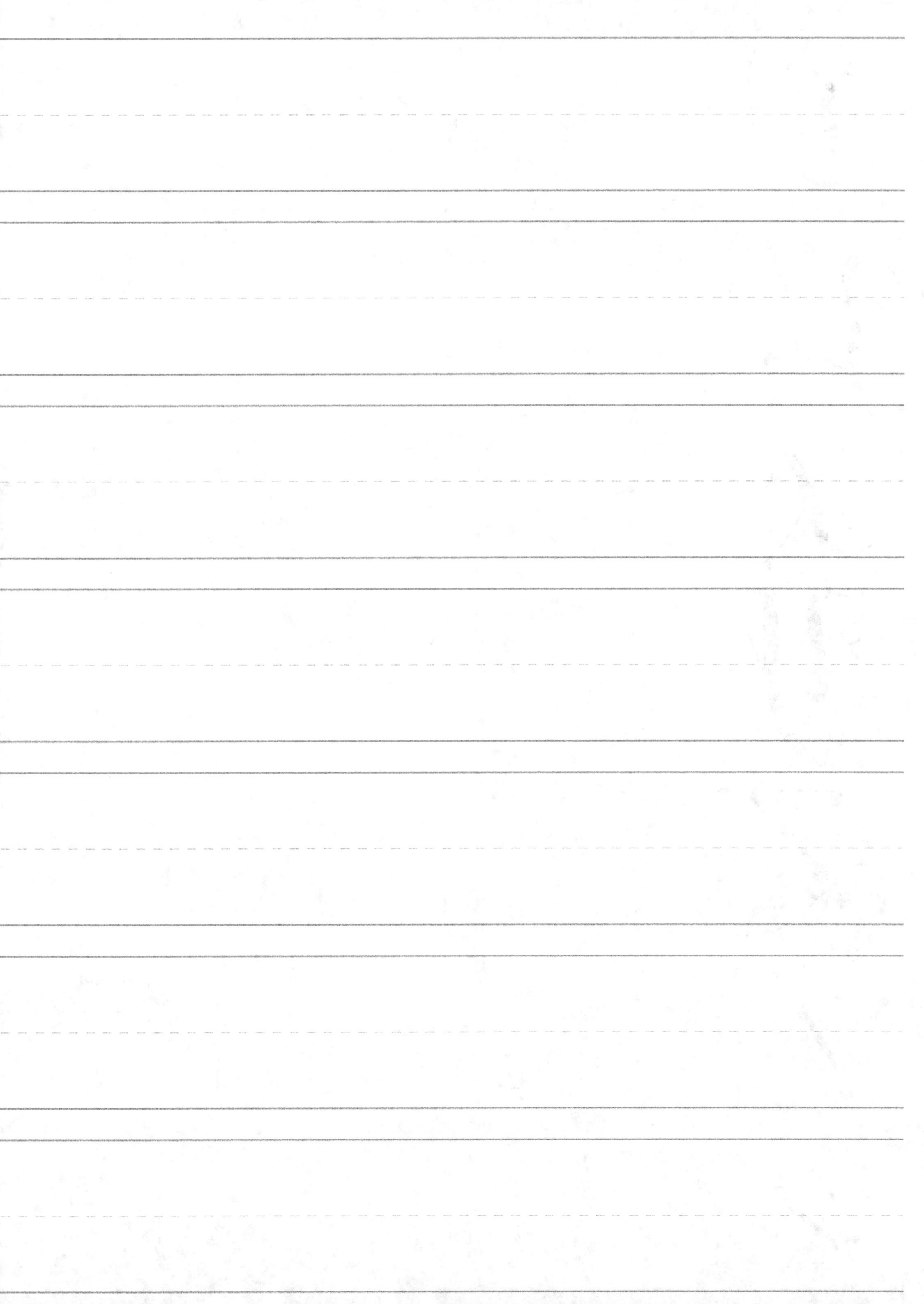

$\mathcal{V}$ $\mathcal{V}$ $\mathcal{V}$

$\mathcal{W}$ $\mathcal{W}$ $\mathcal{W}$

$\mathcal{X}$ $\mathcal{X}$ $\mathcal{X}$

$\mathcal{Y}$ $\mathcal{Y}$ $\mathcal{Y}$

$\mathcal{Z}$ $\mathcal{Z}$ $\mathcal{Z}$

! ! !

? ? ?

a   a

b   b

c   c

d   d

e   e

f   f

g   g

h h

i i

j j

k k

l l

m m

n n

o o

p p

q q

r r

s s

t t

u u

v v

w w

x x

y y

z z

# #

& &

Alphabet Drill 4

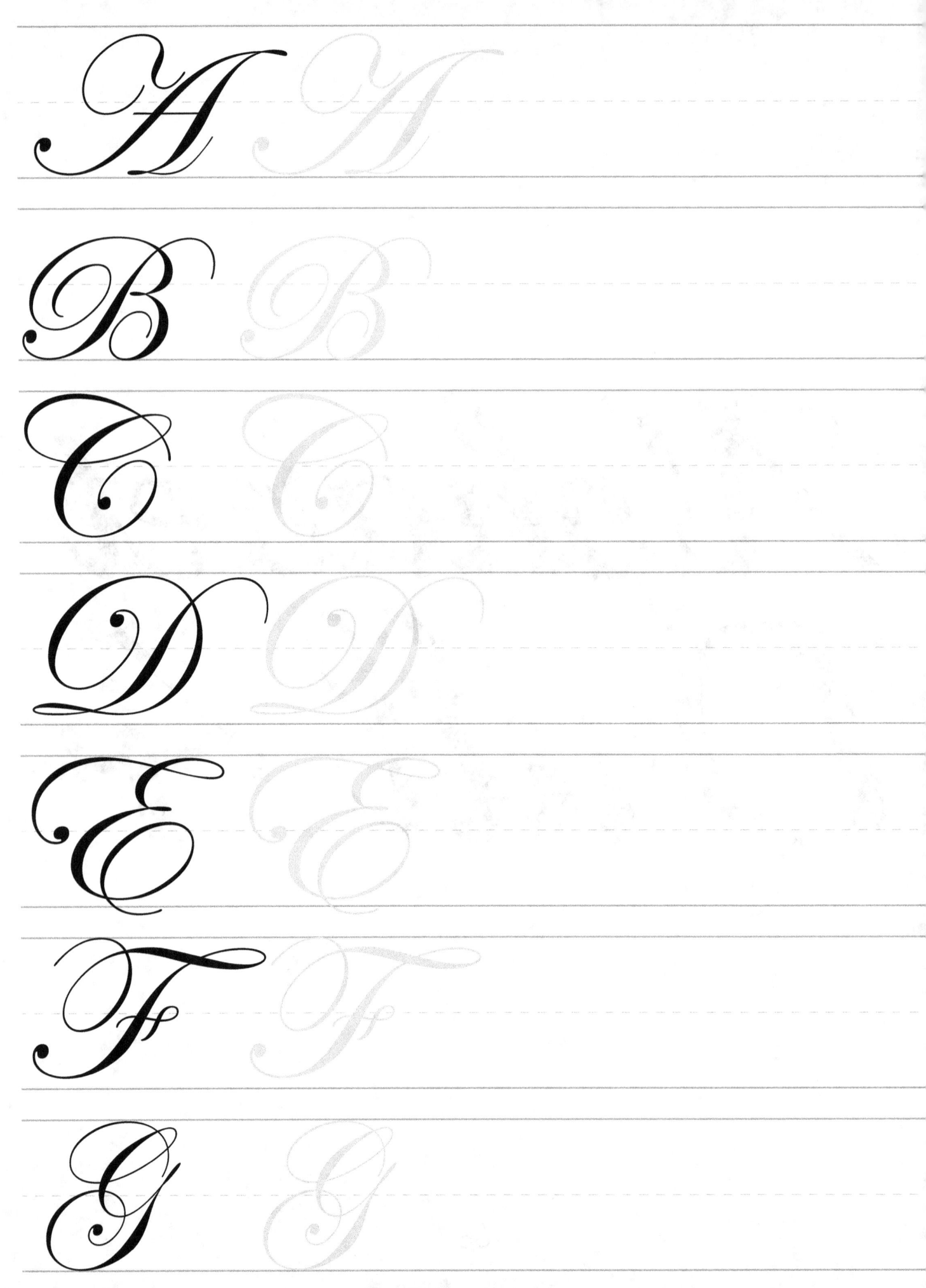

H

I

J

K

L

M

N

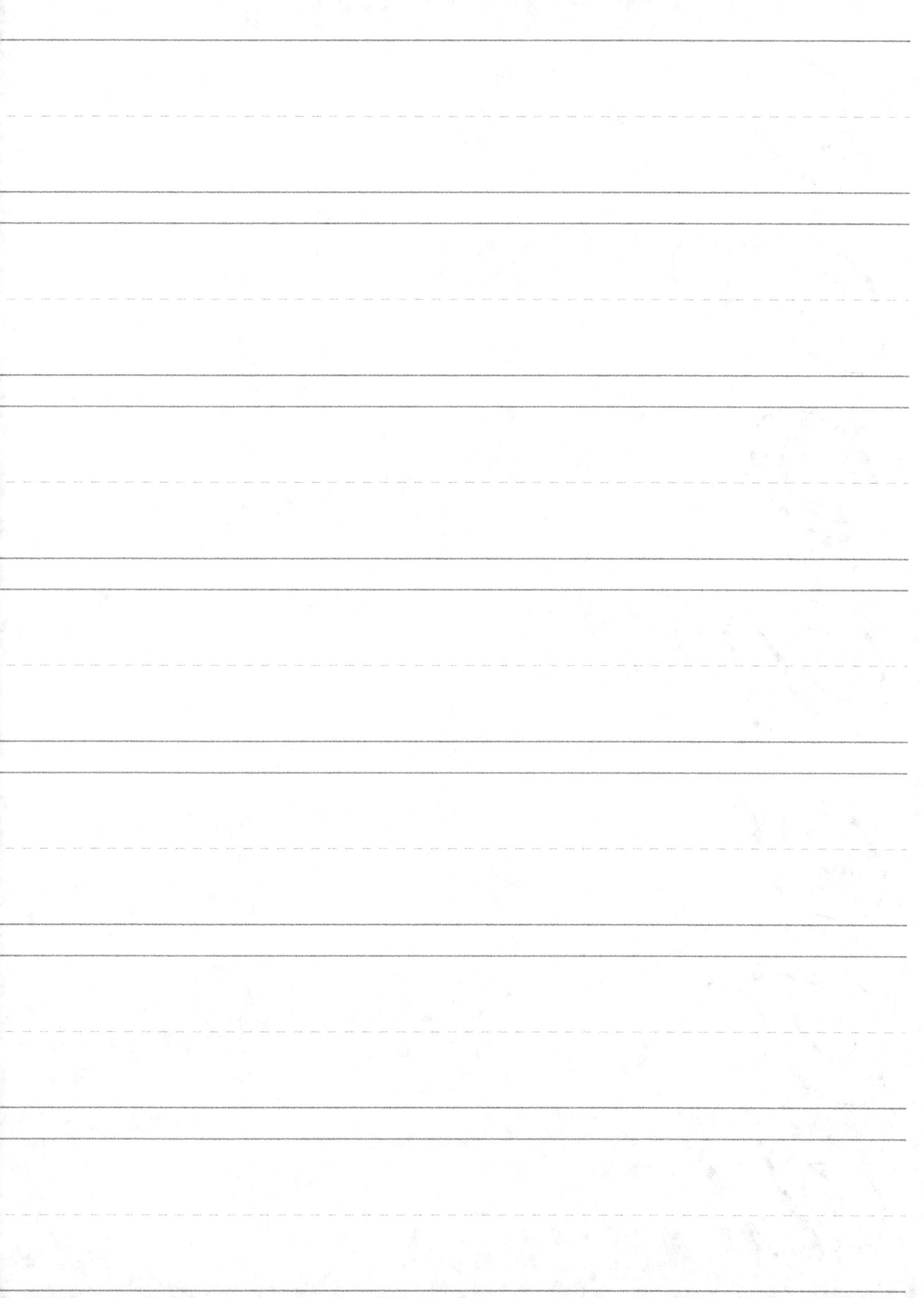

O O
P P
Q Q
R R
S S
T T
U U

$\mathcal{V}$

$\mathcal{W}$

$\mathcal{X}$

$\mathcal{Y}$

$\mathcal{Z}$

!

?

a *a*

b *b*

c *c*

d *d*

e *e*

f *f*

g *g*

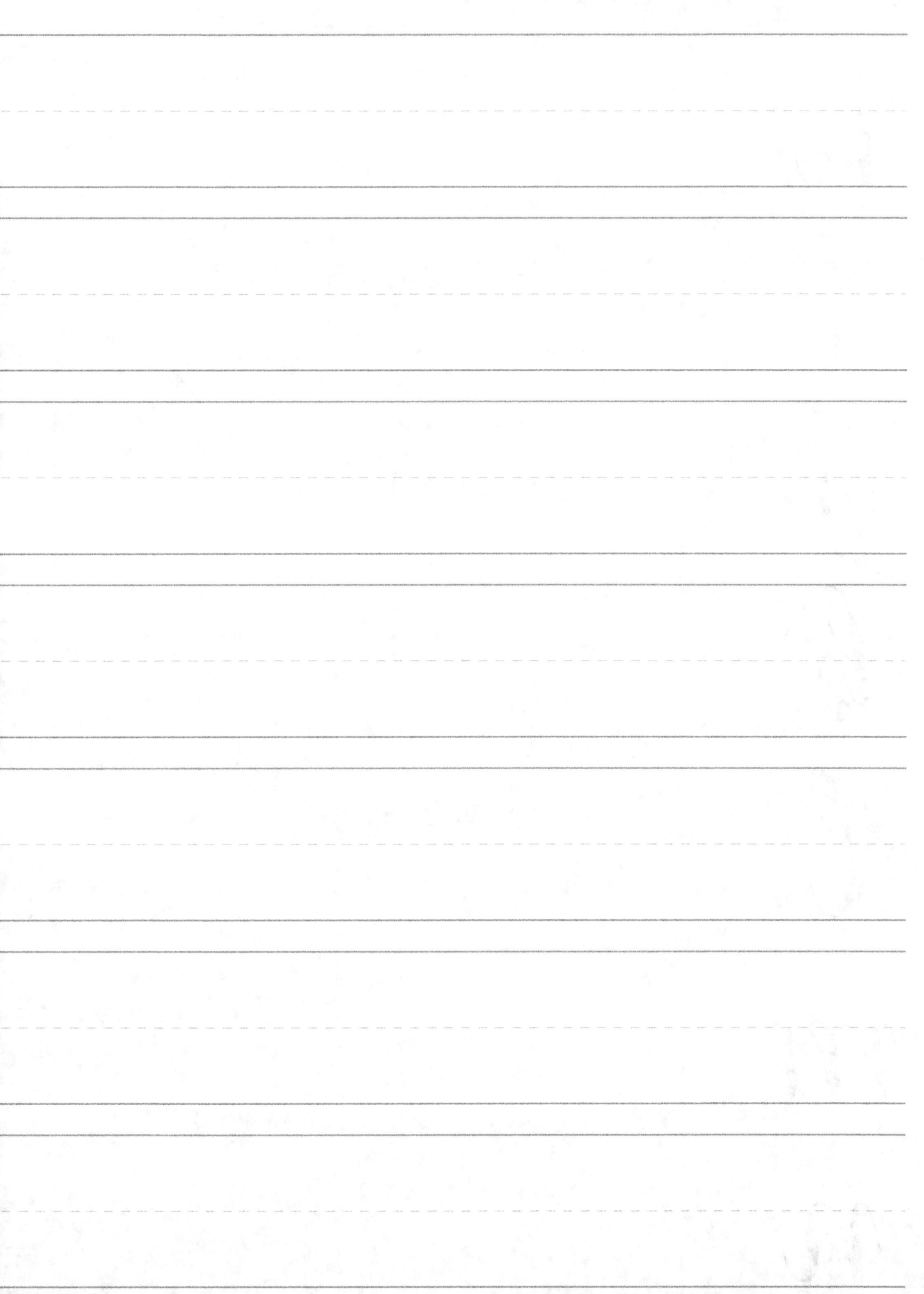

h h

i i

j j

k k

l l

m m

n n

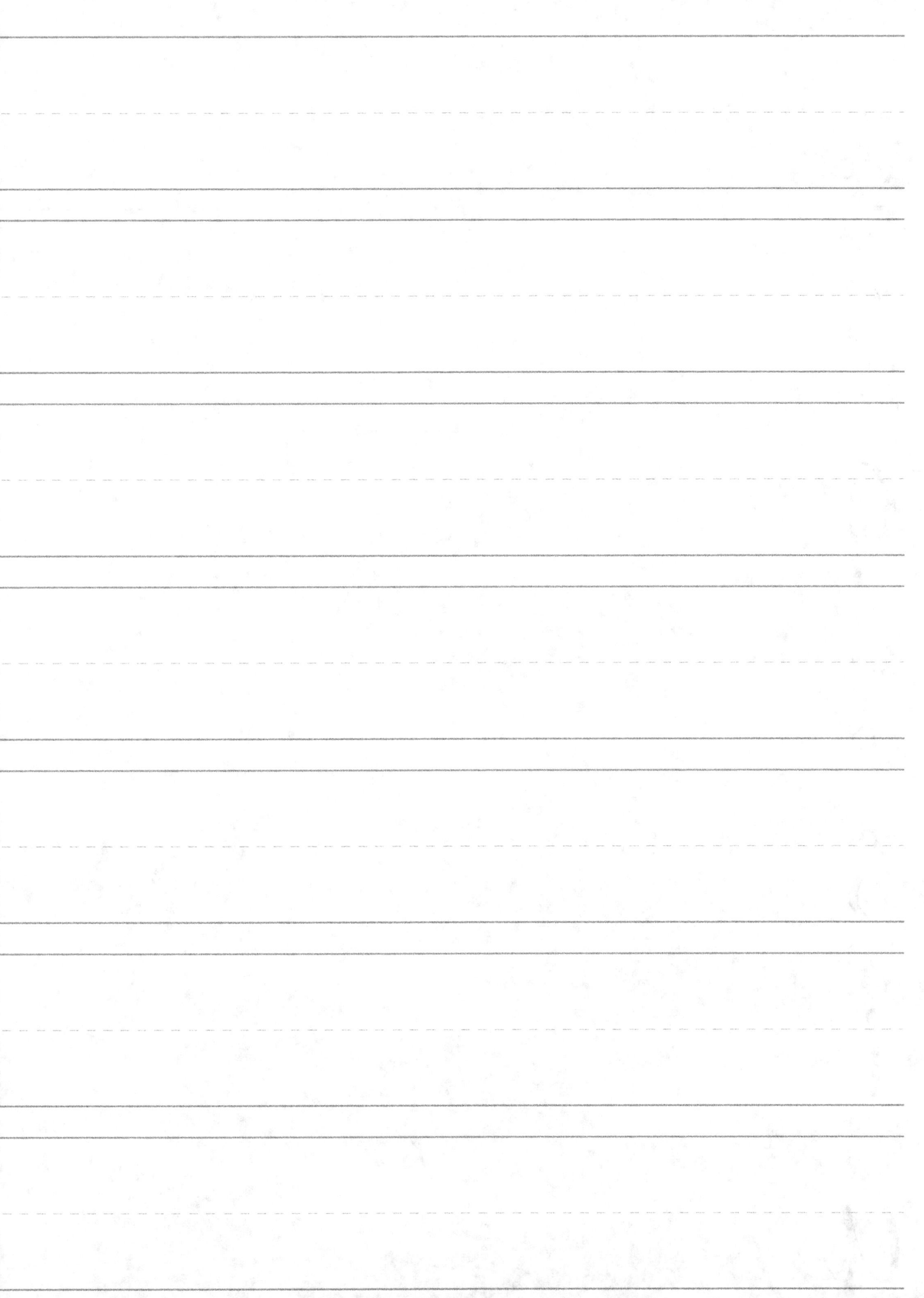

o o

p p

q q

r r

s s

t t

u u

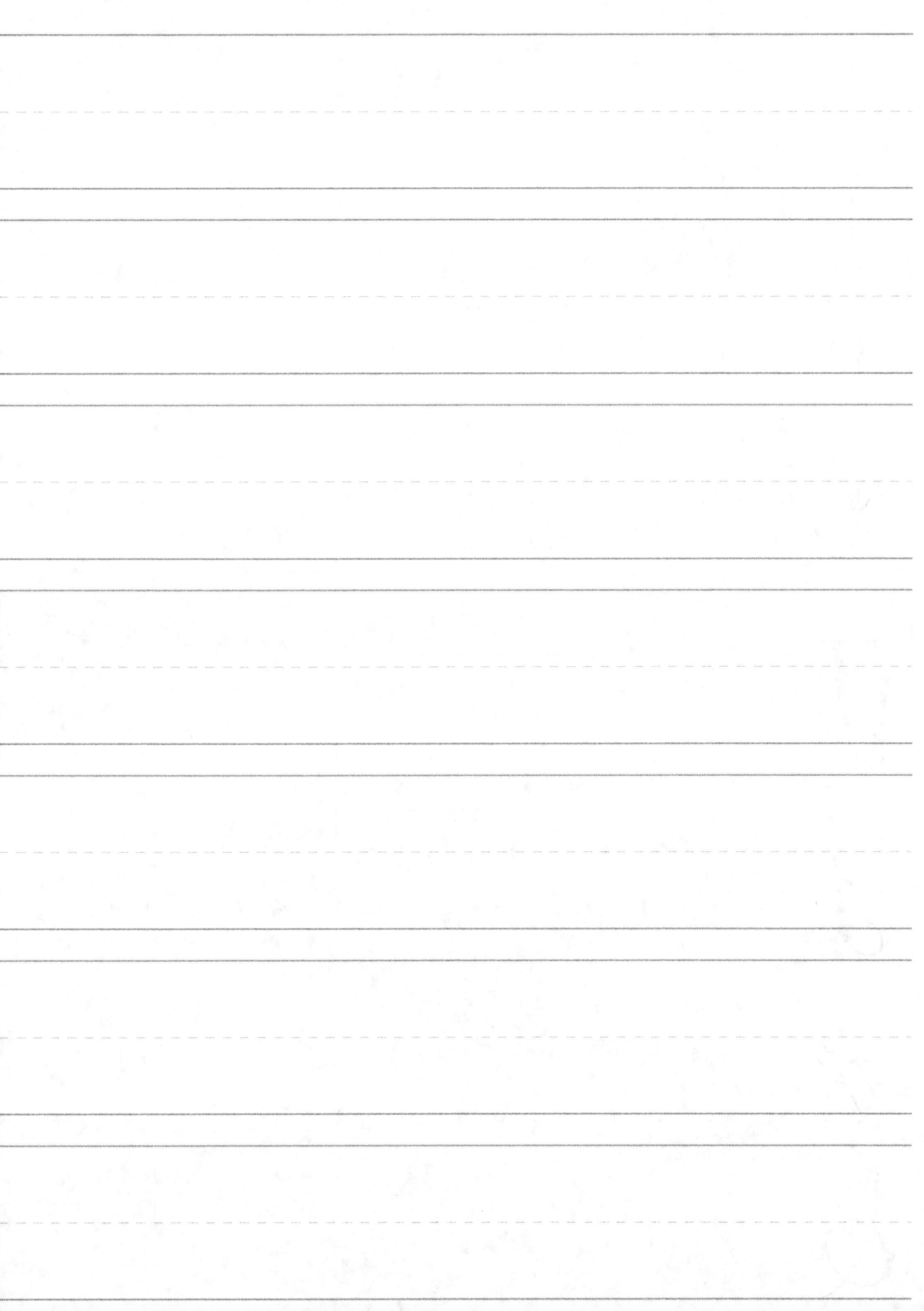

v v

u u

x x

y y

3 3

# #

& &

Connect Letters

CONNECT LETTERS :

Premium

TRACE :

Premium

PRACTICE :

CONNECT LETTERS :

Support

TRACE :

Support

PRACTICE :

CONNECT LETTERS :

Sweety

TRACE :

Sweety

PRACTICE :

CONNECT LETTERS :

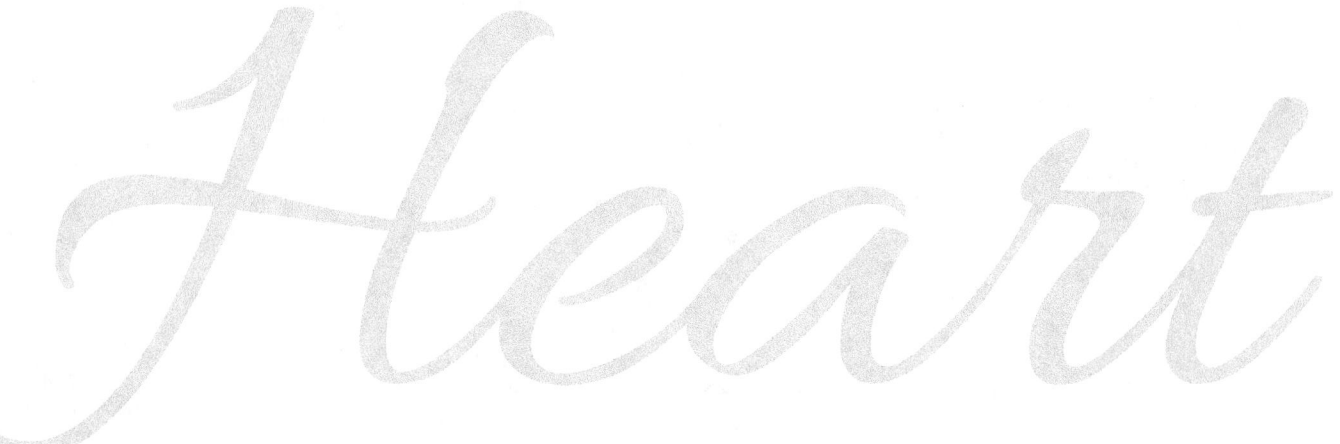

Heart

TRACE :

Heart

PRACTICE :

CONNECT LETTERS :

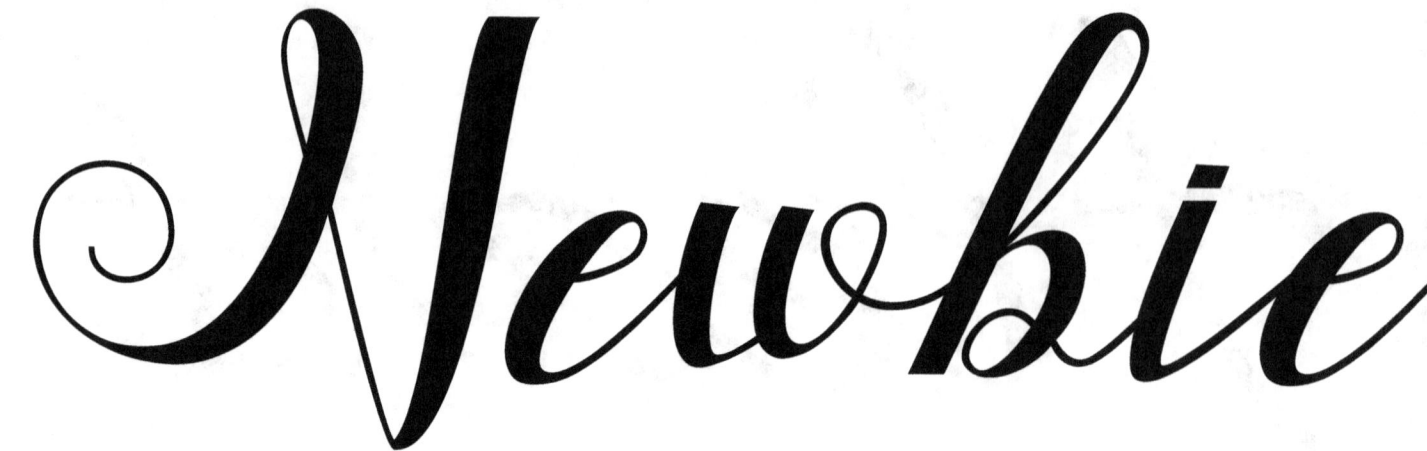

TRACE :

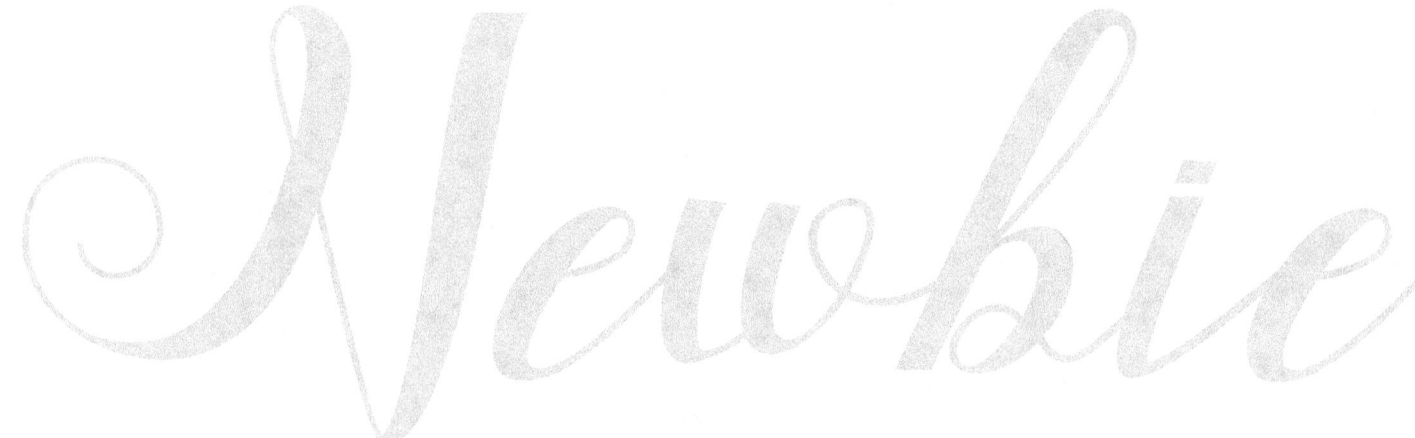

PRACTICE :

CONNECT LETTERS :

Beginner

TRACE :

Beginner

PRACTICE :

CONNECT LETTERS :

Difficult

TRACE :

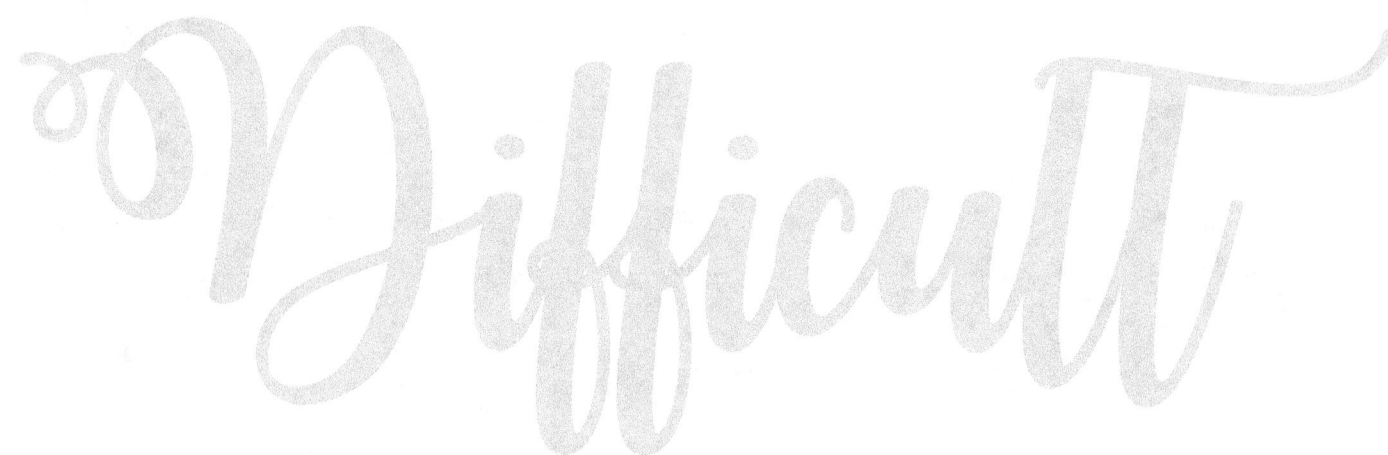

PRACTICE :

CONNECT LETTERS :

Inspriation

TRACE :

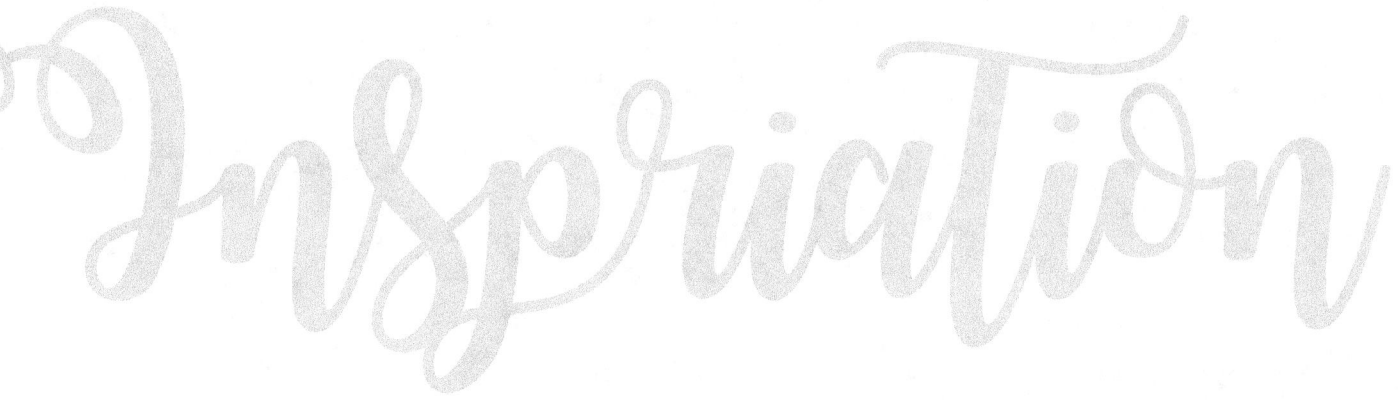

PRACTICE :

CONNECT LETTERS :

Alphabet

TRACE :

Alphabet

PRACTICE :

CONNECT LETTERS :

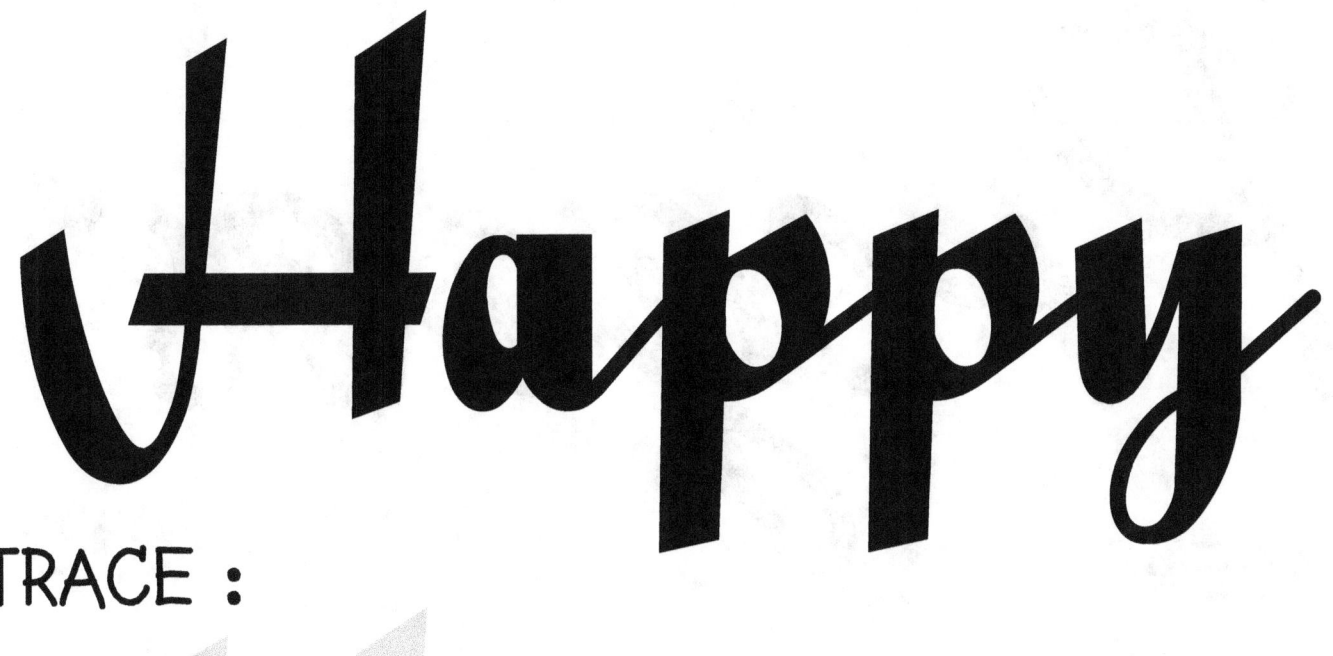

TRACE :

Happy

PRACTICE :

CONNECT LETTERS :

Progess

TRACE :

Progess

PRACTICE :

CONNECT LETTERS :

Bible

TRACE :

Bible

PRACTICE :

Project

&

Practice

PROJECT :

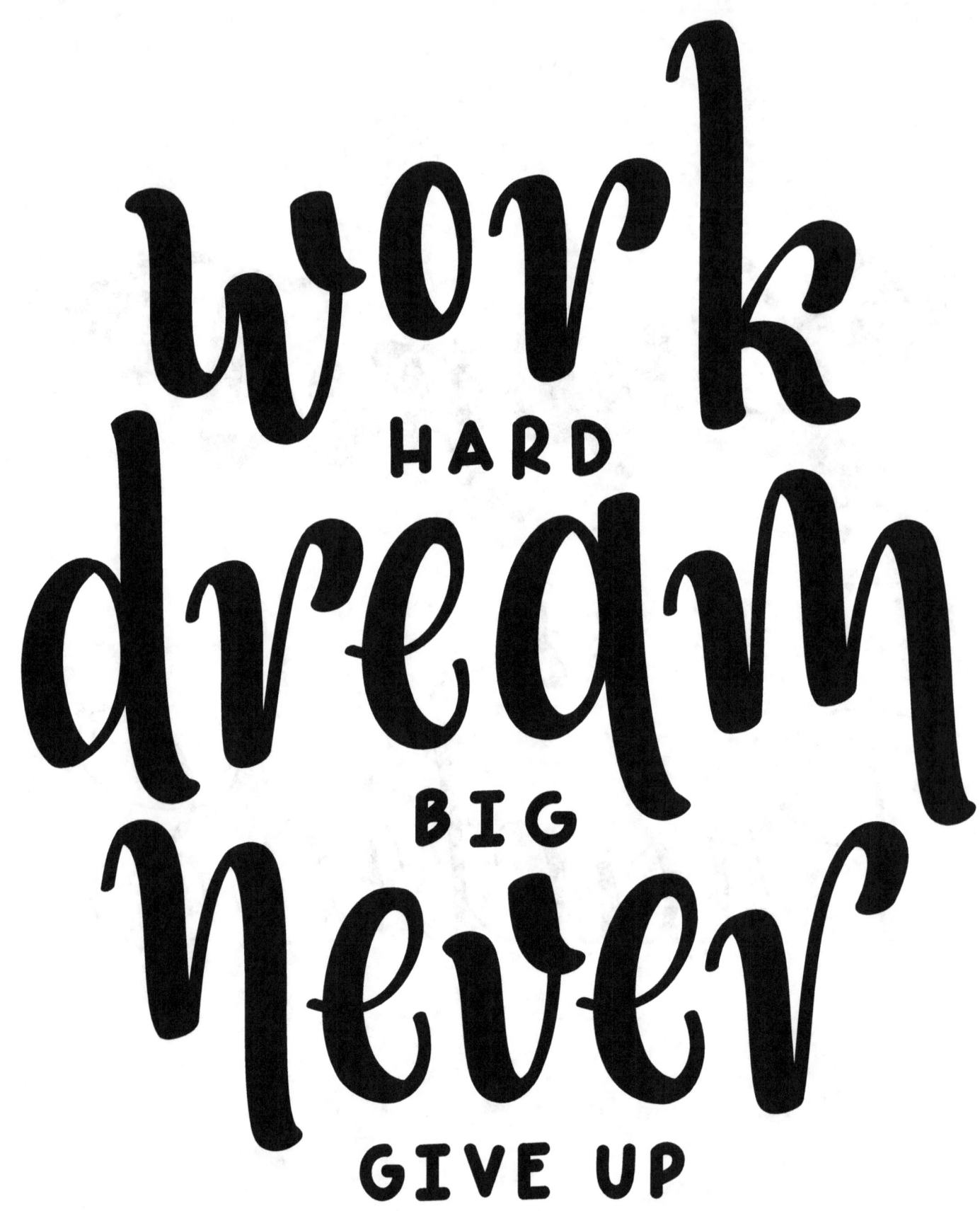

work HARD dream BIG never GIVE UP

PROJECT :

life
IS AN
adventure
BE AN
explorer

PROJECT :

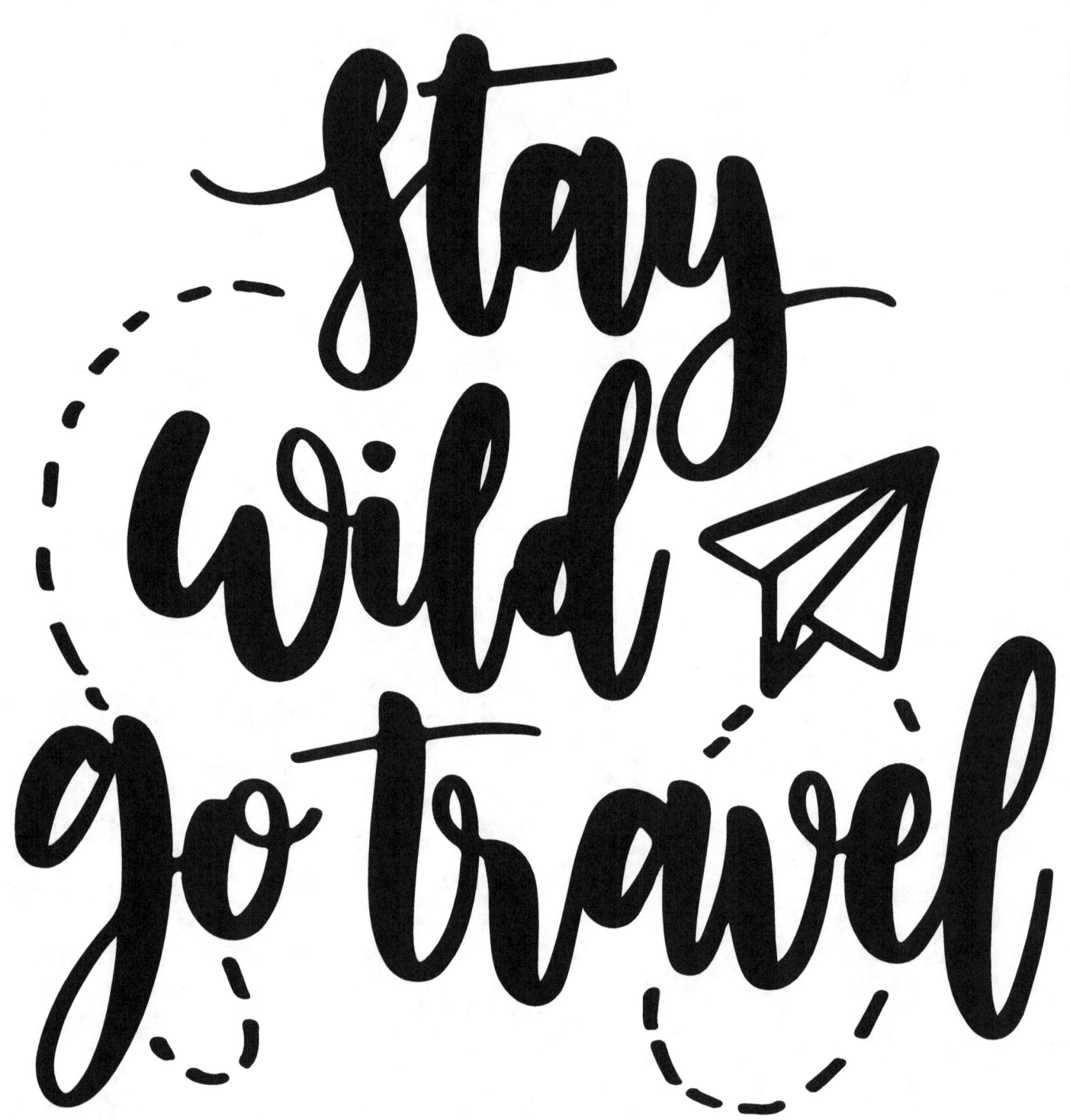

PROJECT :

Hello GUYS!

PROJECT :

thank you

PROJECT :

I like
YOU

www.ingramcontent.com/pod-product-compliance
Lightning Source LLC
Chambersburg PA
CBHW081603220526
45468CB00010B/2753